Book and CD

Really Easy Guitar!

Chords

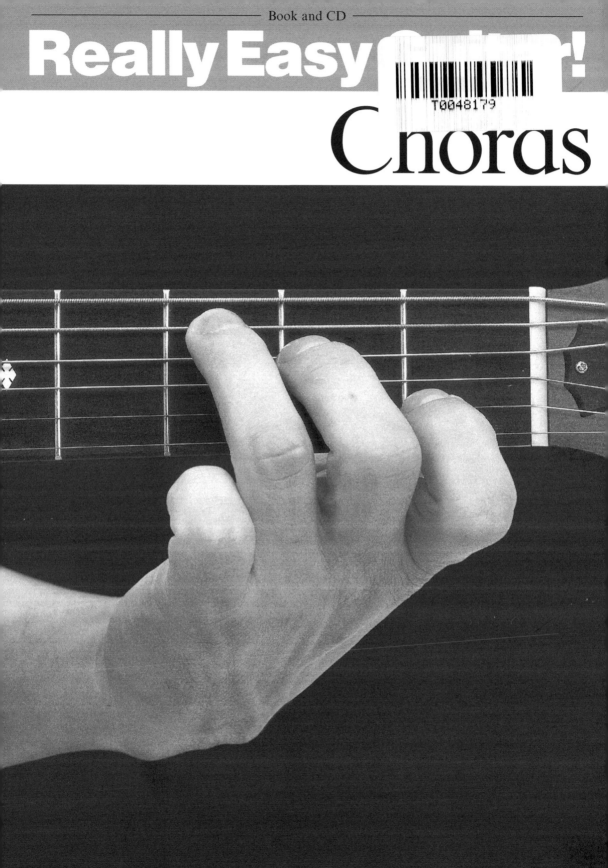

Wise Publications

London/New York/Paris/Sydney/Copenhagen/Berlin/Madrid/Tokyo

Contents

Published by
Wise Publications
14/15 Berners Street, London W1T 3LJ. England.

Exclusive Distributors:
Music Sales Limited
Distribution Centre, Newmarket Road,
Bury St. Edmunds, Suffolk IP33 3YB, England.
Music Sales Corporation
180 Madison Avenue, 24th Floor, New York
NY10016, USA.
Music Sales Pty Limited
Units 3-4, 17 Willfox St, Condell Park,
NSW, 2200 Australia.

Order No. AM969683
ISBN: 0-7119-8773-4
This book copyright © 2004 by Wise Publications

Written and arranged by Cliff Douse
Edited by Sorcha Armstrong
Music processed by Simon Troup
Book design by Chloë Alexander
Photographs by George Taylor

Printed in Great Britain

CD mastered by Jonas Persson
Guitars by Arthur Dick

Your Guarantee of Quality
As publishers, we strive to produce every book to the
highest commercial standards.
The music has been freshly engraved and the book has
been carefully designed to minimise awkward page turns
and to make playing from it a real pleasure.
Particular care has been given to specifying acid-
free, neutral-sized paper made from pulps which
have not been elemental chlorine bleached. This
pulp is from farmed sustainable forests and was
produced with special regard for the environment.
Throughout, the printing and binding have been
planned to ensure a sturdy, attractive publication
which should give years of enjoyment.
If your copy fails to meet our high standards, please
inform us and we will gladly replace it.

www.musicsales.com

Got any comments?
e-mail reallyeasyguitar@musicsales.co.uk

Introduction

Welcome to the *Really Easy Guitar Chords* book, a useful reference for all guitar players.

This book will show you how to play many different chords in each of the twelve keys. It also explains the basic theory that determines how the chords are named.

The accompanying CD features professional recordings of each chord in this book so you should listen to these to make sure that you are playing them properly.

Just follow our three step guide to using this book and you will have an extensive knowledge of chords and the theory behind them in next to no time.

Happy music making!

1 Tune your guitar

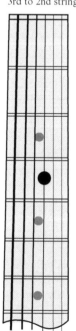

Before you can start to play along with the CD, you'll need to make sure that your guitar is in tune. Track 1 on the CD gives you notes to tune to for each string, starting with the top E string, and then working downwards.

Alternatively, tune the bottom string first and then tune all the other strings to it.

Follow the tuning diagram below and tune from the bottom string upwards.

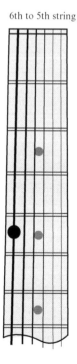 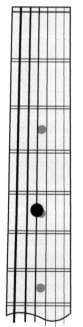 

| 6th to 5th string | 5th to 4th string | 4th to 3rd string | 3rd to 2nd string | 2nd to 1st string |

2 Understanding fretbox diagrams

Throughout this book, fretbox diagrams are used to show chord shapes. Think of the box as a view of the fretboard from head on – the thickest (lowest) string is on the left and the thinnest (highest) string is on the right.

The horizontal lines correspond to the frets on your guitar; the circles indicate where you should place your fingers.

An x above the box indicates that that string should not be played; an o indicates that the string should be played open.

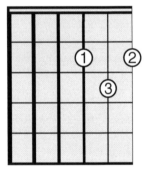

Hence, when playing this chord of D, make sure that you don't hit the bottom two strings.

Shapes that are played higher up the neck are described in the same way – the lowest fret used is indicated to the left of the box. A curved line above the box shows that a first finger barre should be used.

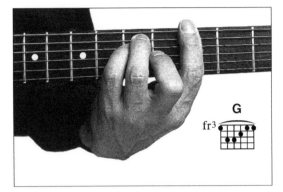

This barre chord of G is played at the third fret, with the first finger stretching across all six strings.

3 Understanding chord names

Chords are built out of triads. A triad is usually made up of any note plus the notes a third and a fifth above it. The four common types of triad are major, minor, diminished and augmented:

TRIAD	INTERVALS			NOTES IN C		
Major	1	3	5	C	E	G
Minor	1	3♭	5	C	E♭	G
Diminished	1	3♭	5♭	C	E♭	G♭
Augmented	1	3	5♯	C	E	G♯

These triads can be extended by adding further notes: a major seventh chord is a major triad with the seventh note of the major scale added, while a minor seventh chord contains a flattened seventh note as well as a flattened third. In addition there are dominant seventh chords, which are major triads with flattened seventh notes. Here is a list of the most common chords built on C, although these formulae can be applied to any root:

	INTERVALS					NOTES IN C				
MAJOR										
C Major ('C')	1	3	5			C	E	G		
C6	1	3	5	6		C	E	G	A	
Cmaj7	1	3	5	7		C	E	G	B	
Cmaj9	1	3	5	7	9	C	E	G	B	D
DOM 7th										
C7	1	3	5	7♭		C	E	G	B♭	
C9	1	3	5	7♭	9	C	E	G	B♭	D
MINOR										
Cm	1	3♭	5			C	E♭	G		
Cm6	1	3♭	5	6		C	E♭	G	A	
Cm7	1	3♭	5	7♭		C	E♭	G	B♭	
Cm9	1	3♭	5	7♭	9	C	E♭	G	B♭	D
OTHER										
Cdim	1	3♭	5♭			C	E♭	G♭		
Caug	1	3	5♯			C	E	G♯		
Csus4	1	4	5			C	F	G		
Cdim7	1	3♭	5♭	7♭♭		C	E♭	G♭	B♭♭(A)	

The chord diagrams in this book show the root of each chord with a reversed circle ❶ or a double circle ◎ in the case of an open string.

A Chords

A

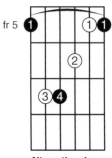

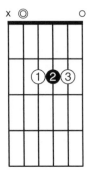

Alternative shape

Am

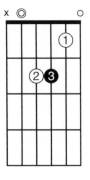

Alternative shape

Asus4

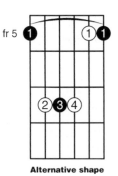

Alternative shape

A5

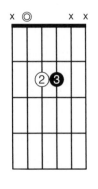

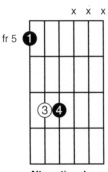

Alternative shape

A Chords

A6

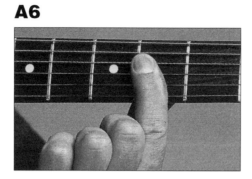

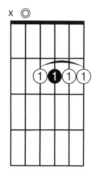

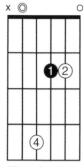
Alternative shape

Am6

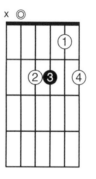

fr 4

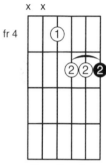
Alternative shape

A7

Alternative shape

Amaj7

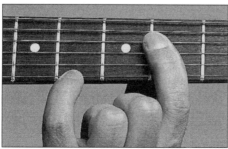

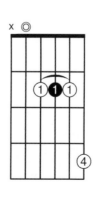

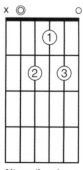
Alternative shape

A Chords

Am7

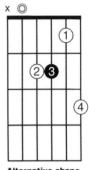

Alternative shape

A7#9

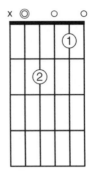

fr 6

fr 11

Alternative shape

Aadd9

fr 5

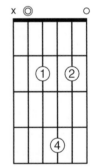

Alternative shape

A9

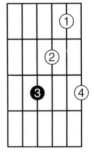

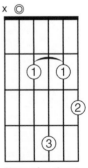

Alternative shape

A Chords

Am9

fr 5

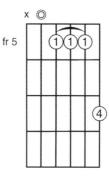

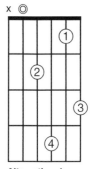

Alternative shape

A11

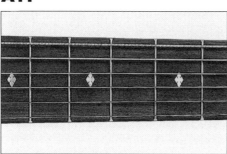

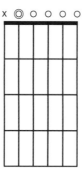

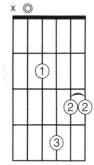

Alternative shape

Aaug

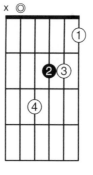

fr 2

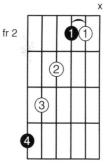

Alternative shape

Adim7

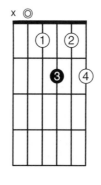

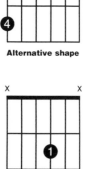

Alternative shape

Bb

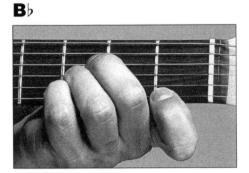

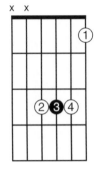

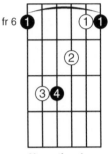

Alternative shape

Bbm

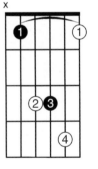

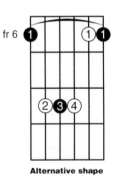

Alternative shape

Bbsus4

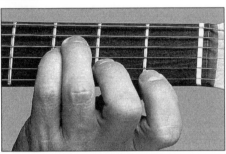

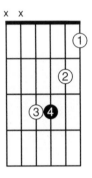

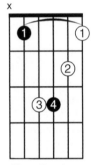

Alternative shape

Bb5

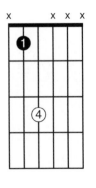

Alternative shape

B♭6

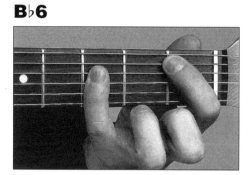

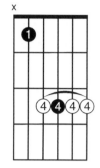

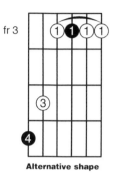

Alternative shape

B♭m6

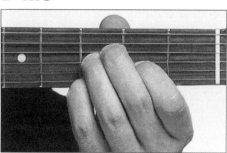

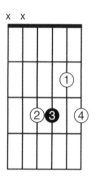

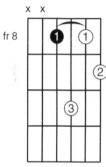

Alternative shape

B♭7

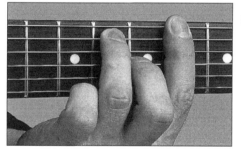

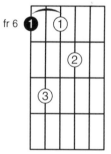

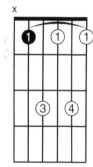

Alternative shape

B♭maj7

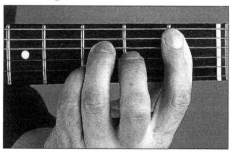

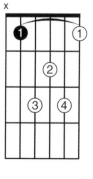

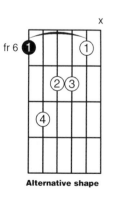

Alternative shape

B♭m7

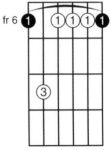

Alternative shape

B♭7♯9

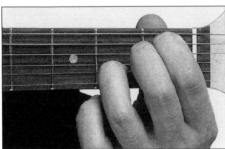

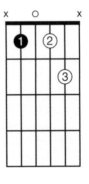

fr 12

Alternative shape

B♭add9

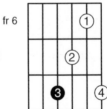

fr 6

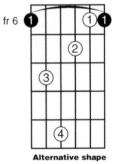

fr 6

Alternative shape

B♭9

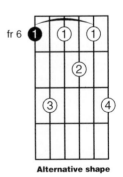

fr 6

Alternative shape

B♭m9

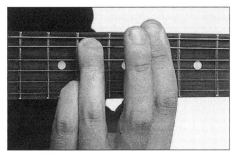

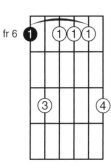

fr 6

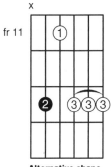

fr 11

Alternative shape

B♭11

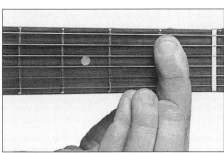

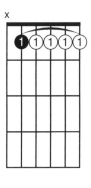

fr 4

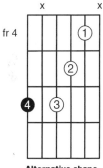

Alternative shape

B♭aug

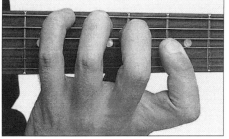

fr 3

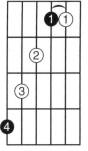

fr 4

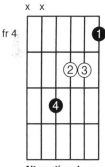

Alternative shape

B♭dim7

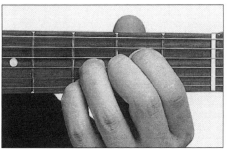

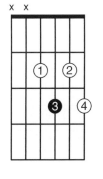

fr 5

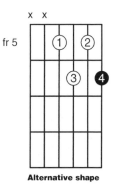

Alternative shape

B Chords

B

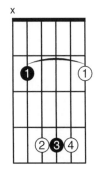

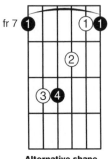

Alternative shape

Bm

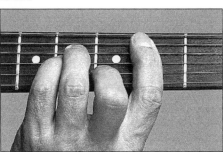

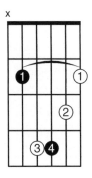

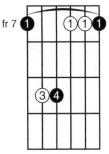

Alternative shape

Bsus4

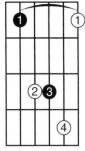

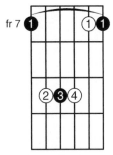

Alternative shape

B5

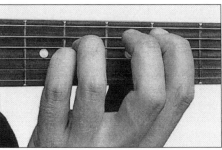

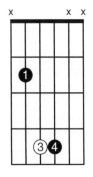

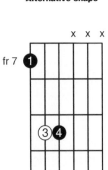

Alternative shape

B Chords

B6

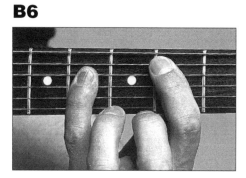

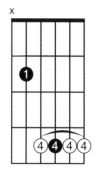

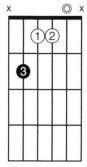

Alternative shape

Bm6

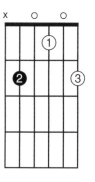

fr 9

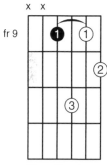

Alternative shape

B7

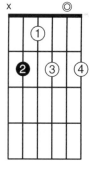

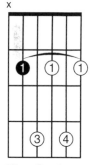

Alternative shape

Bmaj7

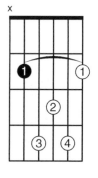

fr 9

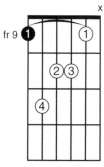

Alternative shape

15

B Chords

Bm7

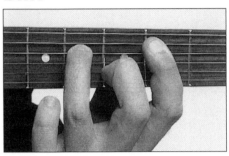
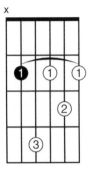
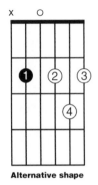

Alternative shape

B7♯9

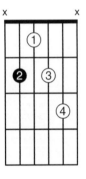
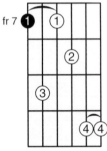

Alternative shape

Badd9

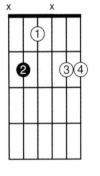
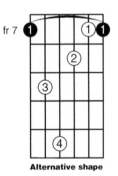

Alternative shape

B9

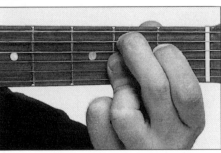
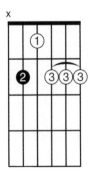
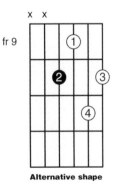

Alternative shape

B Chords

Bm9

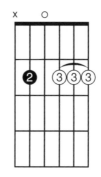

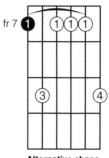

Alternative shape

B11

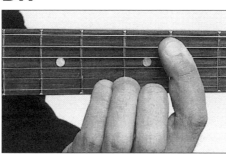

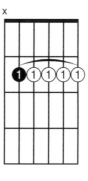

fr 5

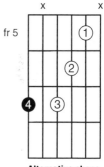

Alternative shape

Baug

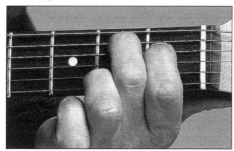

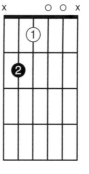

fr 4

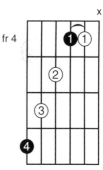

Alternative shape

Bdim7

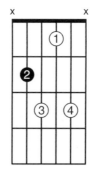

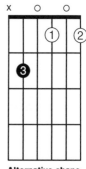

Alternative shape

C Chords

C

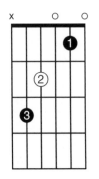

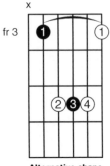
Alternative shape

Cm

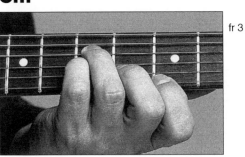

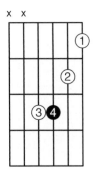

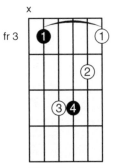
Alternative shape

Csus4

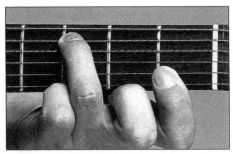

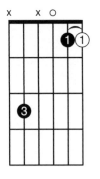

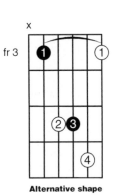
Alternative shape

C5

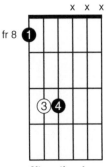
Alternative shape

C6

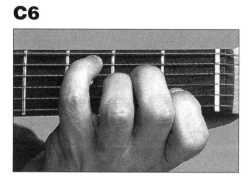

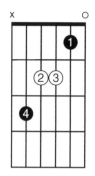

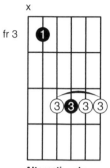

Alternative shape

Cm6

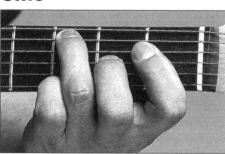

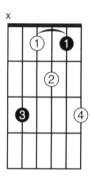

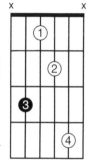

Alternative shape

C7

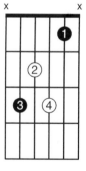

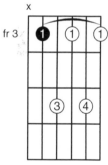

Alternative shape

Cmaj7

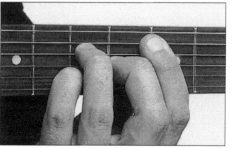

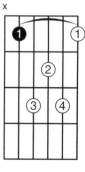

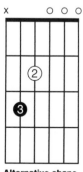

Alternative shape

16

Cm7

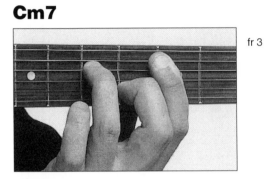

fr 3

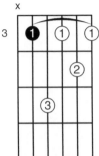

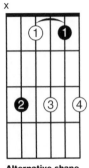

Alternative shape

C7#9

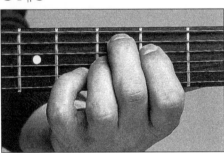

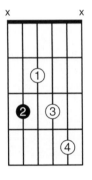

fr 7

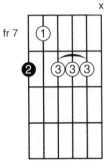

Alternative shape

Cadd9

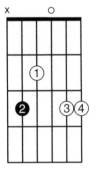

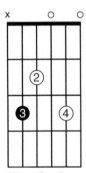

Alternative shape

C9

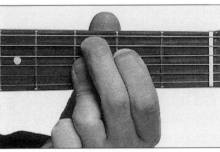

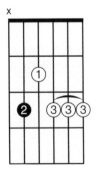

fr 5

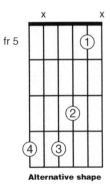

Alternative shape

C Chords

Cm9

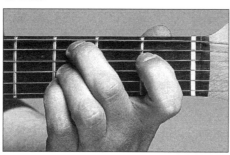

x   x

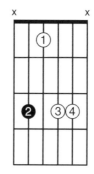

fr 8

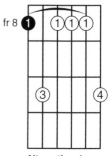

Alternative shape

C11

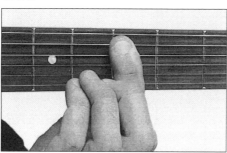

x

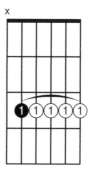

fr 6

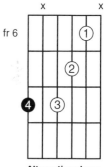

Alternative shape

Caug

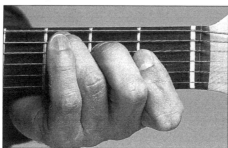

x   x

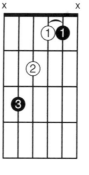

fr 4

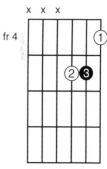

Alternative shape

Cdim7

x   x

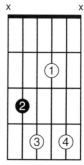

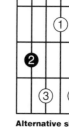

Alternative shape

C♯ (D♭) Chords

C♯

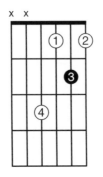

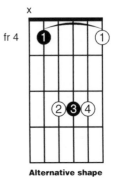

Alternative shape

C♯m

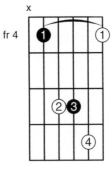

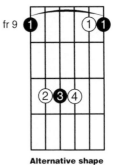

Alternative shape

Csus 4

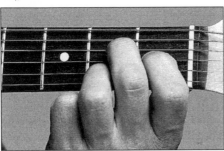

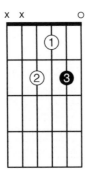

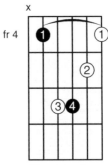

Alternative shape

C♯5

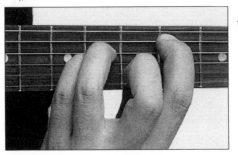

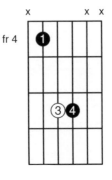

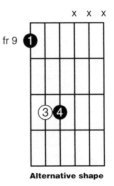

Alternative shape

C# (Db) Chords

C#6

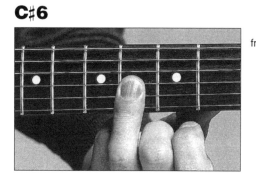

fr 6

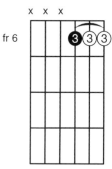

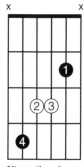

Alternative shape

C#m6

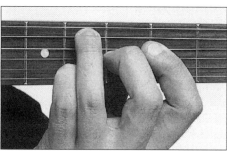

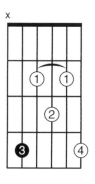

fr 8

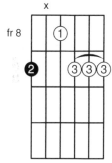

Alternative shape

C#7

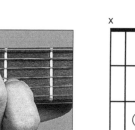

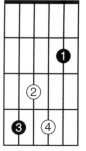

fr 4

Alternative shape

C#maj7

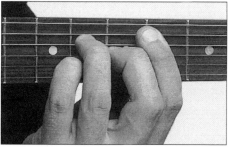

fr 4

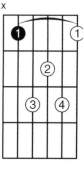

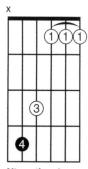

Alternative shape

23

20

C♯m7

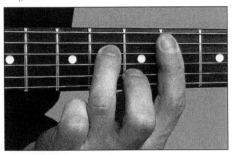

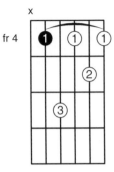

fr 4

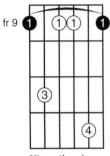

fr 9

Alternative shape

C♯7♯9

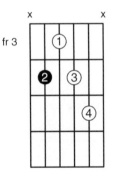

fr 3

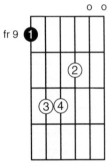

fr 9

Alternative shape

C♯add9

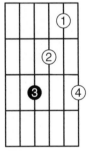

fr 9

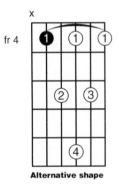

fr 4

Alternative shape

C♯9

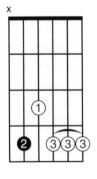

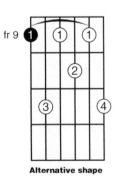

fr 9

Alternative shape

C♯ (D♭) Chords

21

C♯m9

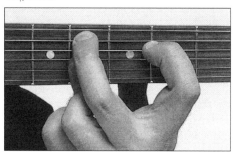

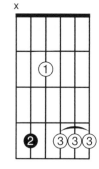

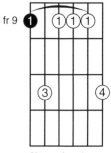

Alternative shape

C♯11

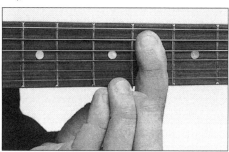

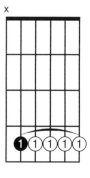

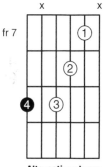

Alternative shape

C♯aug

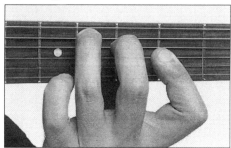

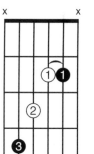

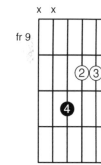

Alternative shape

C♯dim7

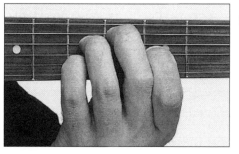

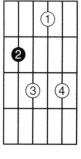

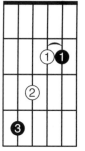

Alternative shape

25

D Chords

D

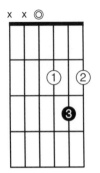

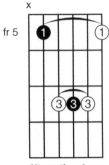

Alternative shape

Dm

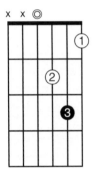

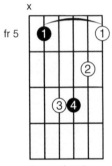

fr 5

Alternative shape

Dsus4

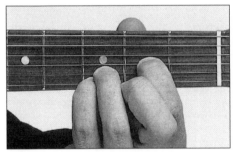

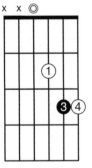

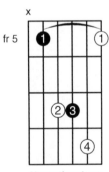

fr 5

Alternative shape

D5

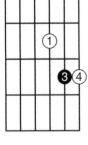

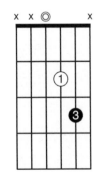

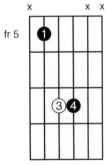

fr 5

Alternative shape

D Chords

D6

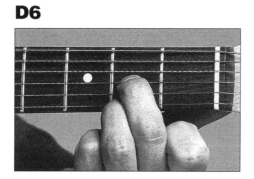

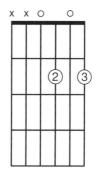

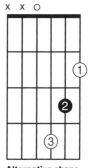

Alternative shape

Dm6

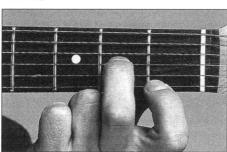

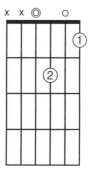

fr 3

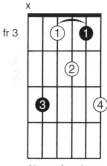

Alternative shape

D7

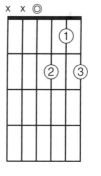

fr 5

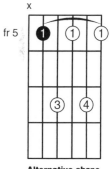

Alternative shape

Dmaj7

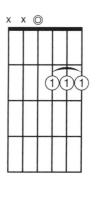

fr 5

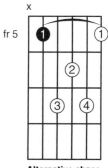

Alternative shape

D Chords

Dm7

x x ◎

fr 5 — Alternative shape

D7♯9

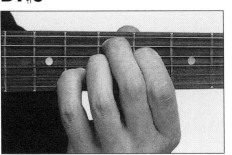

x   x

fr 4

x

fr 9

Alternative shape

Dadd9

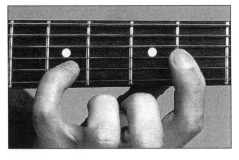

x x ◎

fr 2

x x

fr 10

Alternative shape

D9

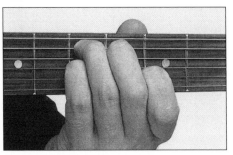

x   O

fr 3

x

fr 4

Alternative shape

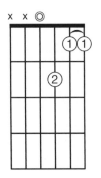
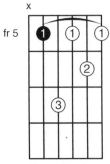
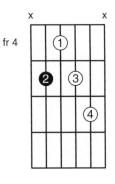
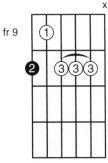
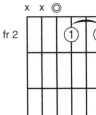
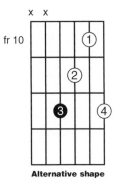
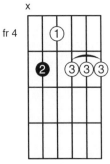

28

25

Dm9

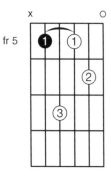

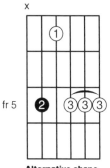

Alternative shape

D11

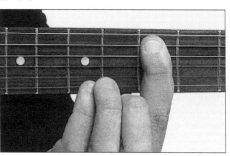

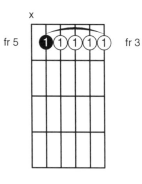

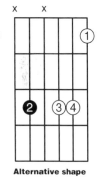

Alternative shape

Daug

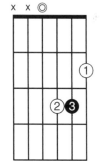

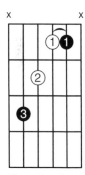

Alternative shape

Ddim7

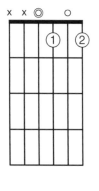

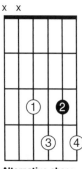

Alternative shape

E♭ (D♯) Chords

E♭

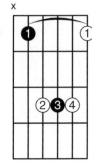
fr 6

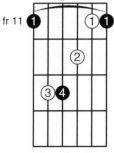
fr 11

Alternative shape

E♭m

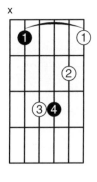
fr 6

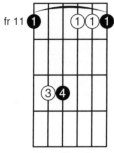
fr 11

Alternative shape

E♭sus4

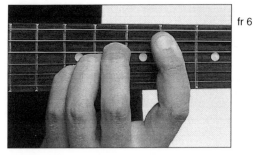

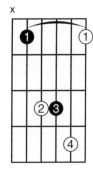
fr 6

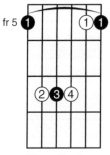
fr 5

Alternative shape

E♭5

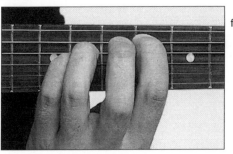

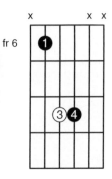
fr 6

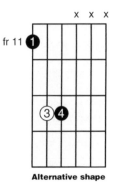
fr 11

Alternative shape

E♭6

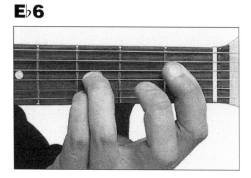

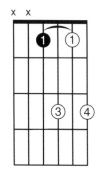

fr 6

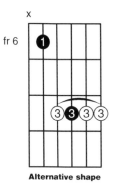

Alternative shape

E♭m6

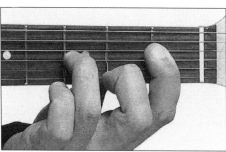

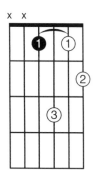

fr 4

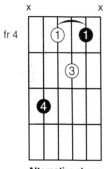

Alternative shape

E♭7

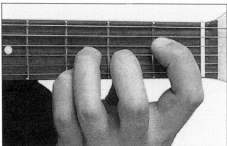

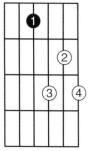

fr 6

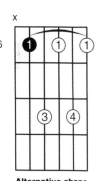

Alternative shape

E♭maj7

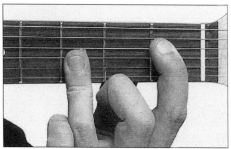

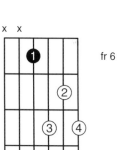

fr 6

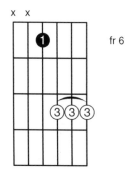

Alternative shape

E♭m7

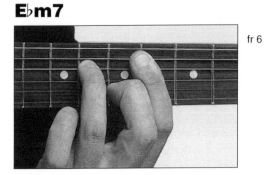

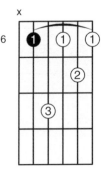

fr 6

fr 11

Alternative shape

E♭7♯9

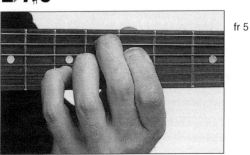

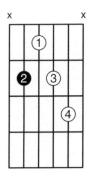

fr 5

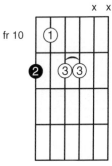

fr 10

Alternative shape

E♭add9

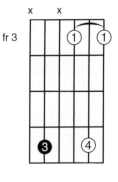

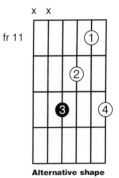

fr 3

fr 11

Alternative shape

E♭9

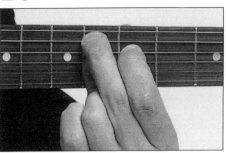

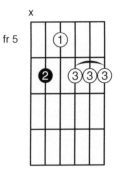

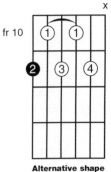

fr 5

fr 10

Alternative shape

E♭m9

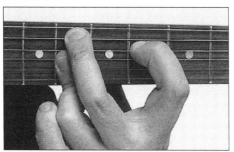

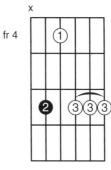

fr 4

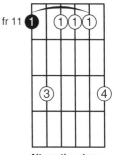

fr 11

Alternative shape

E♭11

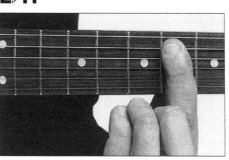

fr 6

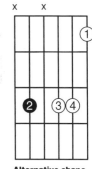

fr 4

Alternative shape

E♭aug

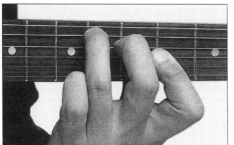

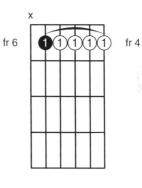

fr 4

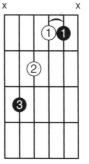

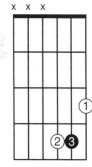

Alternative shape

E♭dim7

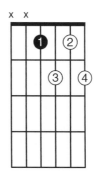

fr 5

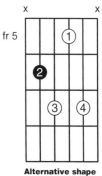

Alternative shape

E Chords

E

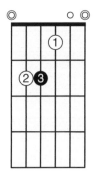

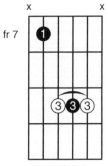
fr 7

Alternative shape

Em

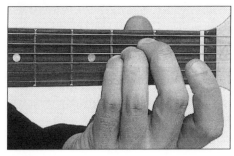

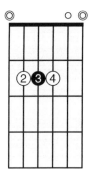

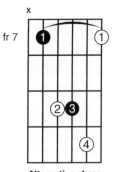
fr 7

Alternative shape

Esus4

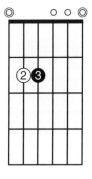

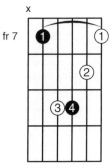
fr 7

Alternative shape

E5

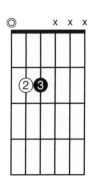

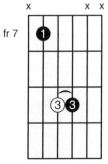
fr 7

Alternative shape

E Chords

E6

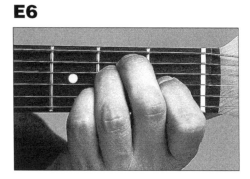

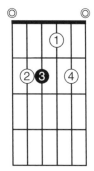

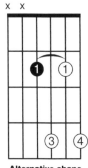

Alternative shape

Em6

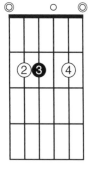

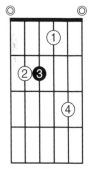

Alternative shape

E7

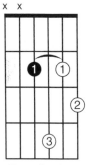

Alternative shape

Emaj7

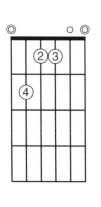

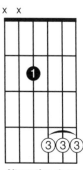

Alternative shape

Em7

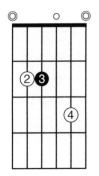

fr 7

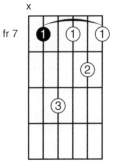

Alternative shape

E7#9

fr 6

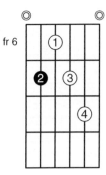

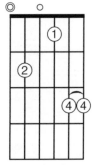

Alternative shape

Eadd9

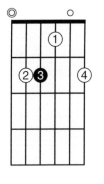

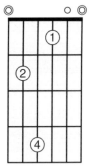

Alternative shape

E9

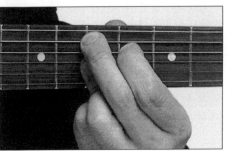

fr 6

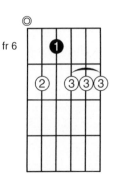

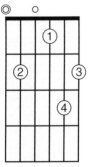

Alternative shape

Em9

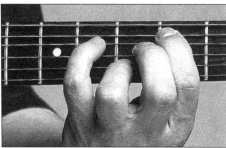

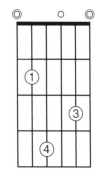

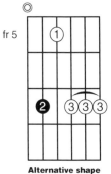

fr 5

Alternative shape

E11

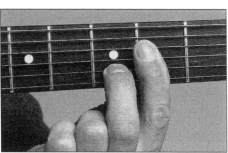

fr 4

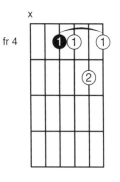

fr 5

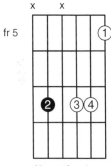

Alternative shape

Eaug

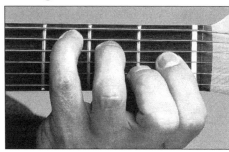

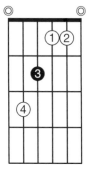

fr 5

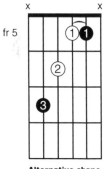

Alternative shape

Edim7

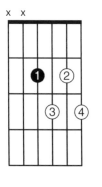

fr 6

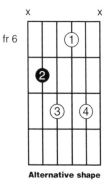

Alternative shape

F Chords

F

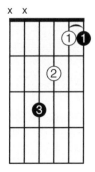
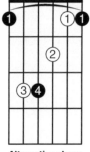

Alternative shape

Fm

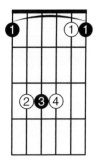
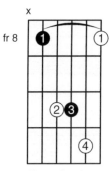

fr 8

Alternative shape

Fsus4

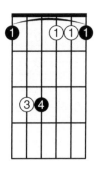
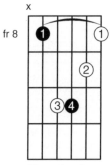

fr 8

Alternative shape

F5

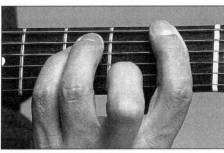
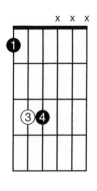
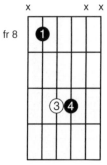

fr 8

Alternative shape

F6

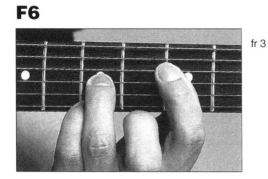

fr 3

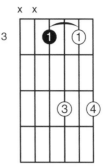

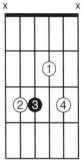

Alternative shape

Fm6

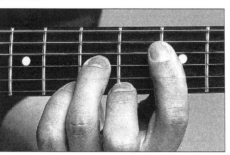

fr 3

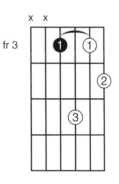

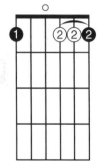

Alternative shape

F7

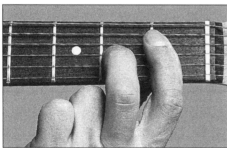

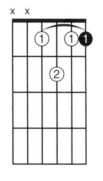

fr 8

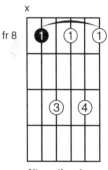

Alternative shape

Fmaj7

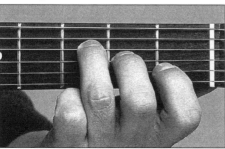

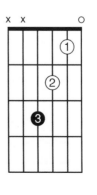

fr 5

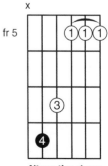

Alternative shape

F Chords

Fm7

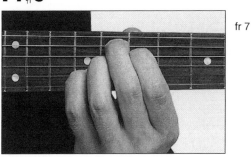

fr 8

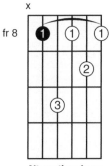

x

Alternative shape

F7♯9

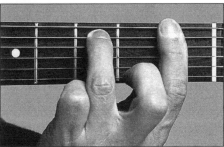

fr 7

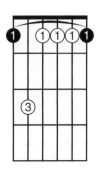

x   x

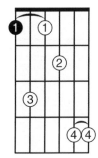

Alternative shape

Fadd9

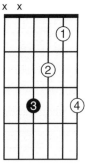

x x

fr 8

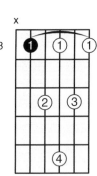

x

Alternative shape

F9

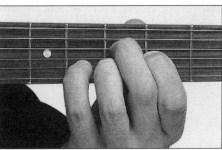

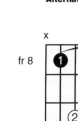

x x

fr 7

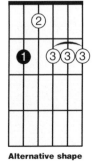

x

Alternative shape

40

Fm9

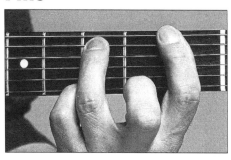

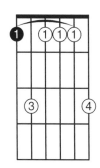

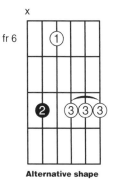

fr 6

Alternative shape

F11

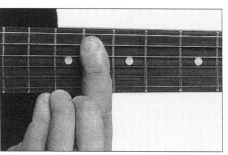

fr 8

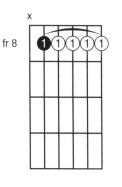

fr 6

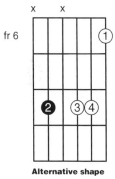

Alternative shape

Faug

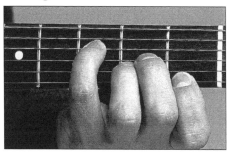

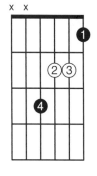

fr 6

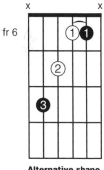

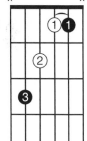

Alternative shape

Fdim7

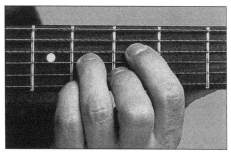

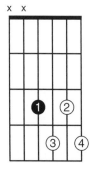

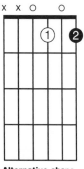

Alternative shape

F♯ (G♭) Chords

F♯

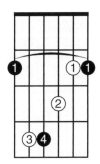
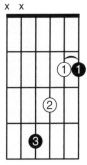

Alternative shape

F♯m

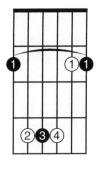
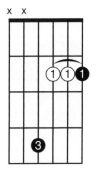

Alternative shape

F♯sus 4

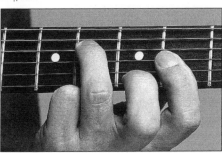
fr 9
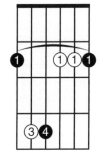

Alternative shape

F♯5

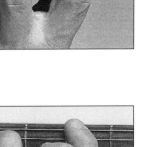

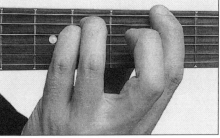
fr 9
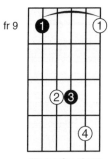
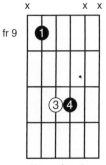

Alternative shape

F♯6

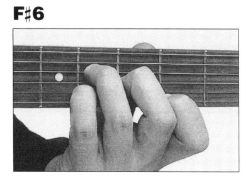

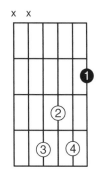

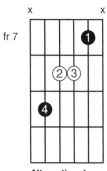

fr 7

Alternative shape

F♯m6

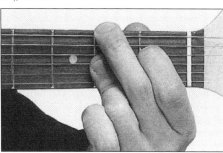

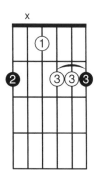

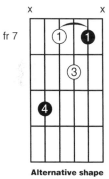

fr 7

Alternative shape

F♯7

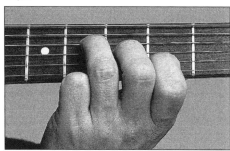

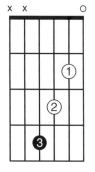

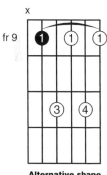

fr 9

Alternative shape

F♯maj7

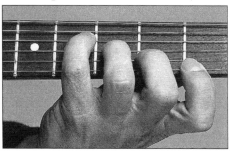

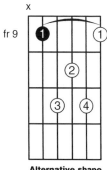

fr 9

Alternative shape

43

40

F♯m7

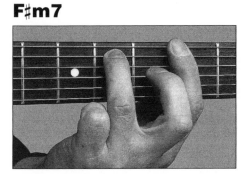
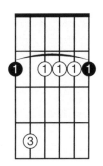
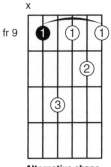

Alternative shape

F♯7♯9

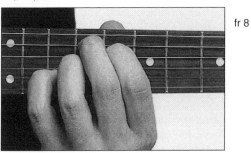
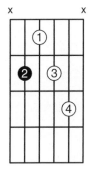
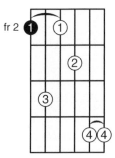

fr 8

fr 2

Alternative shape

F♯add9

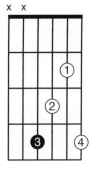
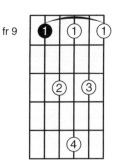

fr 9

Alternative shape

F♯9

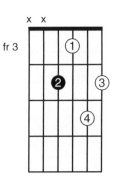
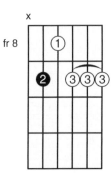

fr 3

fr 8

Alternative shape

F♯m9

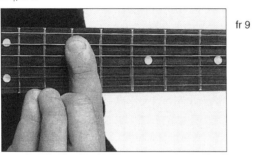

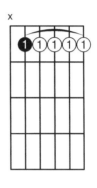

fr 7

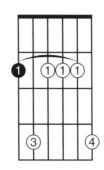

Alternative shape

F♯11

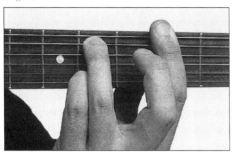

fr 9

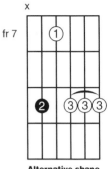

fr 7

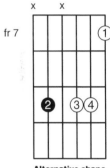

Alternative shape

F♯aug

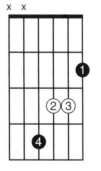

fr 7

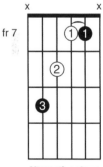

Alternative shape

F♯dim7

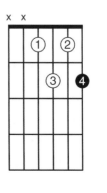

fr 9

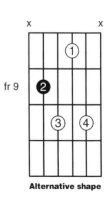

Alternative shape

G Chords

G

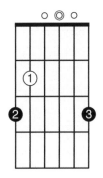
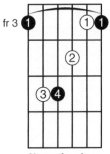

Alternative shape

Gm

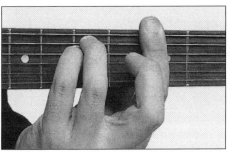
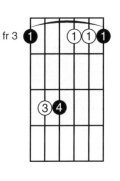
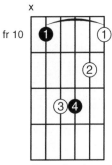

Alternative shape

Gsus4

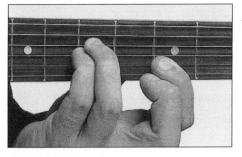
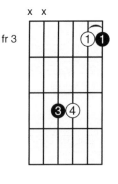
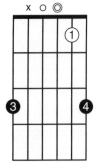

Alternative shape

G5

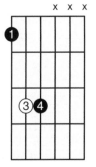
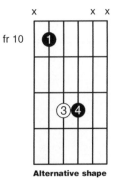

Alternative shape

43

G6

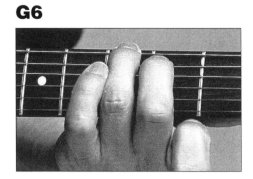

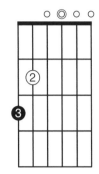

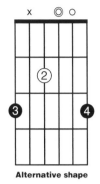

Alternative shape

Gm6

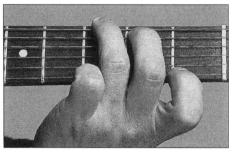

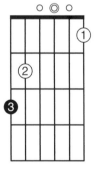

Alternative shape

G7

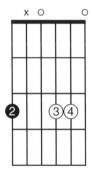

fr 3

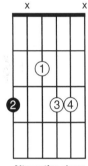

Alternative shape

Gmaj7

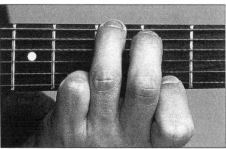

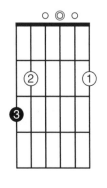

fr 2

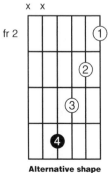

Alternative shape

Gm7

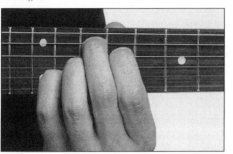

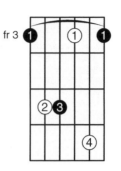

fr 3

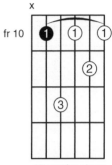

fr 10

Alternative shape

G7♯9

fr 9

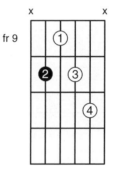

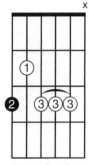

Alternative shape

Gadd9

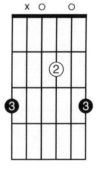

fr 3

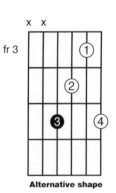

Alternative shape

G9

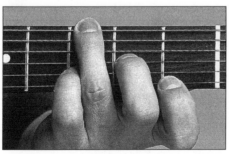

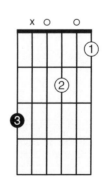

fr 9

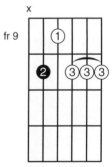

Alternative shape

Gm9

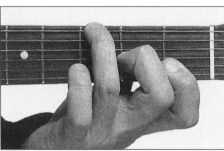

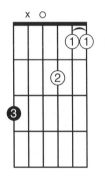

fr 3

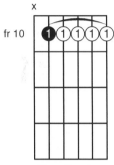

fr 3

Alternative shape

G11

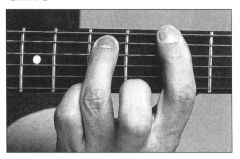

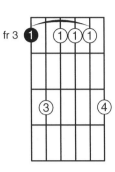

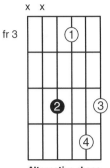

fr 10

Alternative shape

Gaug

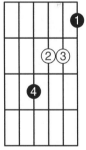

fr 3

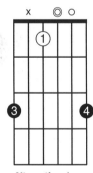

Alternative shape

Gdim7

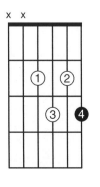

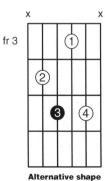

fr 3

Alternative shape

G♯ (A♭) Chords

G♯

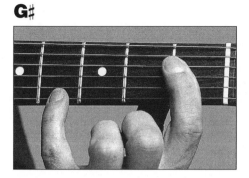

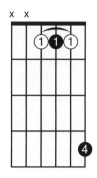

Alternative shape

G♯m

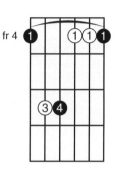

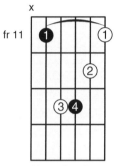

Alternative shape

G♯sus4

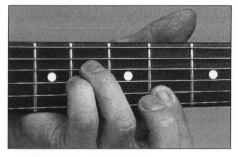

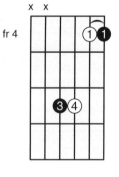

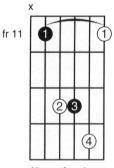

Alternative shape

G♯5

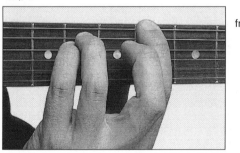

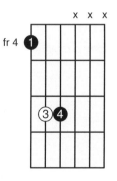

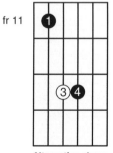

Alternative shape

G♯ (A♭) Chords

47

G♯6

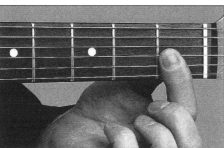

x x x

① ① ① fr 9

x   x

① ② ③ ④

Alternative shape

G♯m6

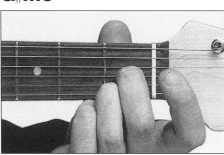

x x x   O

②   ③

x

① ② ③ ③ ③

Alternative shape

G♯7

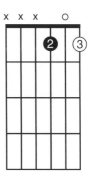

x x x

① ① ②

fr 4   ① ① ① ① ② ③

Alternative shape

G♯maj7

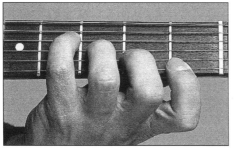

fr 3   x   x

① ② ③ ④

x x x

① ① ③

Alternative shape

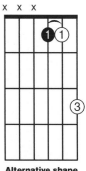

48

G♯m7

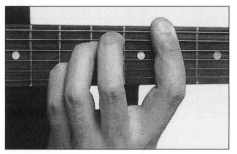

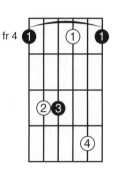
fr 4

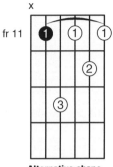
fr 11

Alternative shape

G♯7♯9

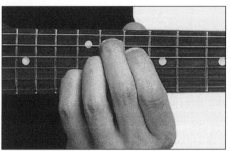

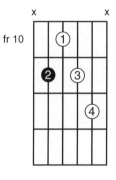
fr 10

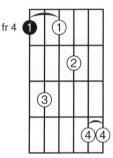
fr 4

Alternative shape

G♯add9

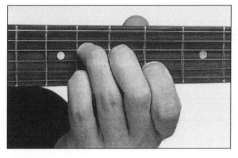

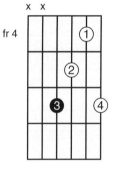
fr 4

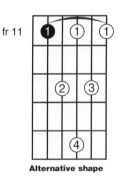
fr 11

Alternative shape

G♯9

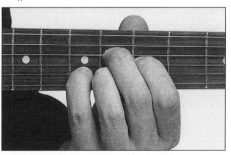

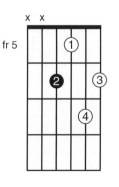
fr 5

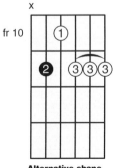
fr 10

Alternative shape

49

G♯m9

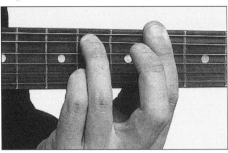

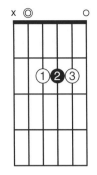

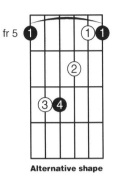

Alternative shape

G♯11

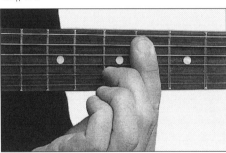

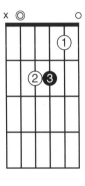

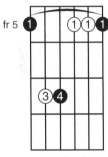

Alternative shape

G♯aug

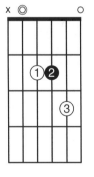

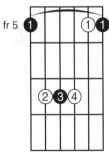

Alternative shape

G♯dim7

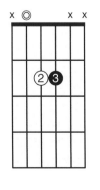

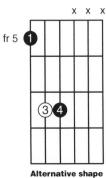

Alternative shape

Slash Chords

D/A

 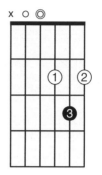 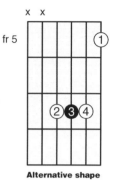

Alternative shape

fr 5

D/B

 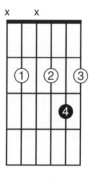 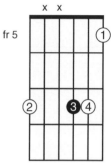

Alternative shape

fr 5

D/C

 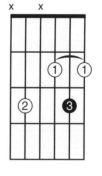 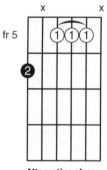

Alternative shape

fr 5

D/E

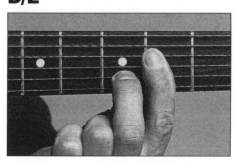 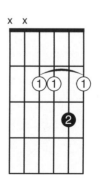 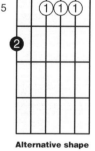

Alternative shape

fr 7